*Rachel Hadas*

# STARTING FROM TROY

DAVID R. GODINE

BOSTON

David R. Godine, Publisher
Boston, Massachusetts

Copyright © 1965, 1966, 1967, 1968, 1974, 1975
by Rachel Hadas

LCC 74-25957
ISBN 0-87923-119-X
Printed in the United States of America

Acknowledgments: some of these poems first appeared in *Harper's Magazine*, *The Harvard Advocate*, *The Lion Rampant*, *The Quince*, and *The Southern Poetry Review*.

A Godine Poetry Chapbook
Second Series

These poems are for my father
Moses Hadas
1900–1966

*ut vultus hominum, ita simulacra vultus
imbecilla ac mortalia sunt, forma
mentis aeterna, quam tenere et exprimere
non per alienam materiam et artem,
sed tuis ipse moribus possis.*

Tacitus, *Agricola*

*Starting from Troy*

## The Fall of Troy

Sing now the heavy furniture of the fall,
the journey's ending. Strong Aeneas bears
deep on his shoulders all the dark wood chairs
and tables of destruction. Bruising, blunt,
they force his feet on up the war-scraped hills
past raped dead temples. All Achilles kills
litters the trail of sofa legs with other
endings of houses. Further up, gods sit
changing their own upholsteries of deceit,
ordaining shelves and benches as the goal
of his dim voyage. Sometimes arrows drawn
on chairbacks point the way they must go on,
signs that some corridor of destiny
is reserving him a threshold. Aeneas weeps
at winds or passion, but steadfastly keeps
carrying battered merchandise marked ROME
in one direction, pondering it all.

## That Time, This Place

All terribly remembered towers of Troy,
this too known house cries out for you.

Priam gone the rest of the sons and daughters
bickering in porticoes reciting
anecdotes by now catalogues of failed
glories slaughters or triumphs lost downtown
half tragedies of cousins scrutinized

fossils of families and fates of war:
the shell remains, the softer parts decay.

How did he say goodbye? what rests with us?
the sad unbaked enamel of the past

no low-relief medallions of farewells
tableaux left unassembled   no forebodings
for framing pictures   did he hope for this?
Undemolished palace, children few, but those
knowing each every weary pore of the others.
Some died down the hill. We go on living.
How well we see our failures!
we know each other's sadness ever better
companionship is what we have and we hate it
we mural of survivors

                       tableaux left unassembled
there on the tower sun in his eyes he said
or in the hall at twilight with wine
something about winning losing going
nothing came after

                         softer parts decay,
the shell remains, and I know every angle
of wall to floor, the smell of all the mornings,
seasons, meals, radiators   Coalesce,
poor jigsaw past, or come apart, poor present.
What here won what battle once upon
and so forth   crickets creaking in the twilight
of unremembered days

                         What rests with us?
How did he say goodbye? Did he say it?
Or must we build what was by tearing down
what is, beat down our celebrated towers
to our own stature, shut our eyes, and sing?

All fighters, fathers, all departed heroes,
our house cries out for you.

## After the Cave

Steaming, with perfume in her hair
of leaves and him as well as myrrh,
Dido stalks out triumphant. He
lingers and watches dew and rain
mixed in the mud and looks at scratched
inscriptions on the rocky wall,
old names with hearts and arrows, and comes out
slowly: her heart feels now the first dark pang.
Why should he come so slowly? And he feels
the weariness of love, untasted since
his fat Creusa, rusty in his strength,
tired of murmurings and muscles, cursing
the emptiness where might have been the gods
to guide him. But the trumpets blast, they go
onward in silence, kingdom into kingdom,
she thinks, and tosses proud her heavy hair
off her brown splendid neck, and wonders what
Anna will say, the feast tonight be like,
the other huntsmen caught.
                            Drums bang: they pass.

## Ode

Eve was waiting for Adam to come and get her.
　　There was no music, but birds
　　made noises calm anticipation
　　　sat easily against, and shadows lay
　　　lightly as ever in interstices.
　　　　Rustlings, sunshine

old and young as the sky that fitted over
　　　the land and down to her feet
　　wove patterns she luxuriated in.
　　No echoes of elaborate unborn
　　　　contingencies yet shimmered through the leaves
　　　　　buglike and humming.

Ah, all the nervous patterns ahead of waiting
　　　suggested themselves, but she
　　sat soft, imperviously open, un-
　　　discrete from lichens at her thighs. Her thoughts,
　　　local in lobes, lungs, fingertips, were not
　　　　such as conjecture

assigns to the creamy creatures who sit in cities
　　　　inwardly vibrant, pulsing.
　　So neither boudoir tidyings of texture,
　　　sweat-scrapings, had eroded her, nor sight
　　　ahead to what would—after sunset—settle
　　　　down to dumb separation, sleep. She sat,
　　　　younger than flowers.

## *Sappho, Keats*

The girls in Lesbos have dark eyes
And scorn to play their natural role.
Flowers don't photosynthesize
On beach and field there, blooming damp
And rich in moonlight. Mushroom-pale
They must have been, but Sappho saw
What flowers blossomed at her feet.
Another nighttime poet sniffed
Instead of looking: cold-stunned eyes
Failed in his fragrant darkness, where
He flew (those viewless wings!) through sweet
Remindful beacons of the air.
I think the impulses were one,
Some rooting down of love, like wheat,
In the unjilting bed of ground.

## Super Nivem
*Asperges me hyssopo, et super nivem dealbabor.*
—Psalm LI

My scars are slow in healing, dark
thin crowns of wound where none should be,
marring what wraps me, marring me.

I am not sad at anything,
not stung, but scars remember more
and make me veteran of a war

I fought forgetting. Stencilled on
wide unresisting planes of skin,
they trace my alphabet of sin,

the language undeciphered still.
But clotted letters I can read.
They mark the parts of me that bleed.

## The Color-Blind Raspberry Picker

A ticklish hedge of bracken
rustles: among the brambles
buzzing with flies he stumbles.
Eyes drowned in lushness sicken
at such arrays of fruit.
Green or red, all rot.
Thorn-pricked muscles slacken.

Swollen, asymmetrical,
unintelligibly hanging
heavy with juices, longing,
tiny ball by ball,
but to be plucked and broken,
each heart of sweetness taken,
they yet refuse to fall,

these berries. Stop or go?
No colors, only weight
to signal sour or sweet.
Dumb densities allow
this to be ripe to come,
that palely hanging on.
He has to touch to know.

'My blindness pushes in:
spotted with pulp I sweat
more juice than I could eat.
But every sugar stain
baked by the sun to crust
is eloquent of waste
and undiscerning gain.

'The moral of my sally
on such remorseless bushes?
Their pallor or their blushes,
personified and silly,
were all I had to trust
as augurs for the feast
for my blind socket belly.'

## Cambridge April

Morning is to reorganize the world!
Light; one red wall; blue day.
Prophetically above us
*La Lutte Continue.*
The sheet is saffron yellow. Milky flesh.
Mr. Matisse with apolitical
intention has walked this room
admiring or creating.

That place to lie in unavoided sunlight
was more than underneath the revolution.
We are inside it. In its red digestion
something bigger is growing.

Also it's April and the shorter nights
give way for what are now called confrontations,
quiet dialogues, mouth to wet late mouth.
It finally stops and we fall into a bed that will brighten
strangely again in the sun.

                        So I'm learning
at least a new way to get used to the idea of mornings.
Always a fresh flag flapping from some high window,
red, unexpected; perhaps on every pillow
an undeciphered face in the dawn before distinctness
makes it impossible to imagine starting over.

## *Daddy*

These weeks, and up and down, and it goes on.

Stay off it for six weeks, one said.
No. Only pulling at the past
can bring me up to what is dead.
Let me write elegies at least,
I said, and then wrote nothing down.

But no forgetting. Elegies
were all around me: youth and age together
or some botched love or any reaching out
meant you and me and death. No need to write.

Breaking the silences and spaces took
more than the violence of time. A fierce
loneliness pushed us in and out of town.
Country and city: what we fled would follow.

Dead people, no, they don't come back.
That's why they're dead, one said.

It pulled together slowly. What must be
still disentangled was the reason first
for seeing things at all
                      so far away
and never further than my arms and legs
and never coming back. No, no forgetting.
It would be funny, if I loved you less,
life's lavish spread of food for elegies.

## *Merry-Go-Round*

So let's all climb on again,
make the great creaking wheels begin
their peeling off of brown to green.

Striped canvas spinning: season, span,
axis and solstice, now and then,
stripe the round world with gold and green.

Churning again to muddy flow
the winter ground too hard to feel,
we gash a wound for sun to heal.

Climb on the back of the past and go,
spheres turning past us high and low,
this creaking carousel of spring:
last call! the world begins again.

## *Daughters and Others*

Zelda Fitzgerald began to see
people as ants and felt afraid.
Lucia Joyce said scornfully
'They buried father, but he's not dead.
He's watching us all.'

Shishkebab of paternal heart
Sylvia gladly would have eaten.
Skewered flesh, rejected blood,
of such stuff those songs were written.

Sylvia's died when she was eight.
How could it be enough to hate?
Love's appetite is unappeased
and I was seventeen.

Daddy, Daddy, shaped in fingers,
nestled unbecomingly
in grumbles, glooms, impatiences,
somehow a blurred blueprint lingers.

Blessing or curse of what might then have been,
the point is what is unsubtractable.
They buried father, but he's not dead.
He's watching us all.

You clever ladies, dead and mad,
fathered and husbanded by fame
(was that it?) that you never had,
scorched by an incandescent name,

or flailing at what put you here
to suffer and create like them,
you stayed as naughty as the cute
precocious girls you all had been,

lavishly smeared them with the gay
sulfurous colors of your wit,
Indian givers, pretty bitches.
And your eyes were all alike:

bright, moist, vulnerable,
always untrusting, slewing back
for some approval from the wings.
You have it now, you know:

biographies swelled fat
on each premenstrual peeve
will make you pin-up martyrs
for future women's movements—

not an inconsonant fate.
Smash that father!
Scrunch that hubby's smug skull
with the frying pan you cook his breakfast in!
Uproot, abolish, triumph.

What stern, indulgent wraith will be on hand
to scold and slap and kiss you afterwards?
They buried father, but he's not dead.
He's watching us all.

## Among Ruins

Upstairs in the museum
guards breathe, glass is dim,
reflecting, everything is hard to see,
tragic and precious therefore. It must be
raining outside. I do not look back.
Across damp marble is someone following?

Today M gave me back the key.
Locked in alone, I begin to understand
the comfort, the relief of spies and spying.
Tomorrow, my escort unspecified,
I shall report myself to the police.
They understand everything one is doing.
Not working, not embezzling from the state
if we lie late enough loving.

I am not sure this is Greece.
Children's voices sound the same from any ground-
    floor window.
Someone is even whistling what sounded like
    'Moon River.'
The dirty boys with icons almost give it away,
but perhaps all this is a conspiracy,
I too a spy: what I will have extracted from my stay
whenever a coded interval is over
is what I have been sent here to discover.

## *Madame Swann at Home*

From the darkening park, from behind the trees,
late sun steals into the salon,
gilds the chrysanthemums at her knees
coppery, and is gone.

The lighted windows and the tea,
the perfume floating in the hall,
gray footmen looming, had to be
ideally inaccessible.

A house is magic only when
one's unimaginable joy,
tasted, grown dull, revives. I thought
it did one rainy day,

but now, initiate once more,
invited to the wrong boudoir,
I smell the flowers at the door
and cultivate my sweet despair.

*Afterword*

Landscape across twenty years of suppers,
mine because mine no longer. Probably
my first ideas came out of what I saw there
not looking. Now I look in them to find:
now they are gone.
Each time a leaning backward,
hunger of memory. When I feel a world
empty of want, this bookcase will be empty.

Two cycles, and our trees grow from your bones.
But rawness is as sure, and a sharp edge revisits
what we grew out of.
Stirred by the cutting out from underneath
of pieces of my making—call it blood
that brims this way with rediscovered loss.

I sit back out of sight, see through the window
the now boxed books being hustled into a truck,
headed for new careers on Staten Island.
They lose their family and keep their life
the way books do.
Back at the house meanwhile time takes me with it.
Already I have lines around my eyes,
maybe from watching things fall back.
Soon spaces in these shelves across the table
will be easy to face as morning. I let go.

## *Mornings in Ormos*

### I

Our wakened voices make the kitten cry.
Unlocked, she tumbles out to kiss our feet.
You haven't looked at me yet.

Sky hides its face from windows small as this one.
Only fierce swaying in the wheat outside
reveals the wind, Ruth in the corn, the wildness.

Down to the sea, the clattering oil-pocked stones,
wandering bottles, *chiudere, aprire*,
mismatched boots, hiss of waves,

a drowned explorer. I am walking east
and the sun, unmoved, has risen.

## II

Morning again. Stop crying.
Donkeys are braying, men are weighing fish,
hammering boats in the shade, Panayítsas fixing his nets,
ten of their children died and his wife is smiling.

Before we slept last night the wind from Russia
was suddenly winter foghorns on the Hudson
when I was small in my bed at the back of the house
protected by my sister's breathing near me.

Such tunnelly sad sounds, long underground,
surfacing now, the mystery quenched in morning,
Albertine dead, the brightness out of reach—
I think about the past and fear the future,

but another old man is coughing in the garden,
Pappagállina shuffles in with frankincense
for Ayios Panteléimon the healer,
I clutch your kindness and sit up to the sun.

## *Landlady*

'God rest your father *hília Saváta*,
a thousand Saturdays,' says Pappagállina
if I draw water for her, wind her wool,
cut her old horny nails.
'God rest him and excuse him.'

So generous a gesture of forgiveness
for an alien's precious dead
lends a dimension to the drippy candles
she offers to her saints.
But all's not myrrh and frankincense.
Now as she virtuously scrubs
a pair of ancient pee-eroded bloomers,
she mutters imprecations at a brother
who called her half a century ago
*scrófa* (teeth grind here). Called her *poutána*!
Never in those same thousand Saturdays
will she forget, it seems. Saint Nicholas
darken his eyes and rip his tongue out,
teach him to call her that!
Cripple him, shrivel him!
All men are pigs.

See Saint Someone's church there on the hill?
Last year she filled the bottles with fresh oil,
whitewashed the walls, dusted all the icons.
He'll listen to her prayers, wait and see.

I listen. Power and belief like these
need less stretch of soul to be acknowledged
than incantations hardly worth the wasting
on the anonymous dead.
She shuffles through the windy summer evenings
hawk-faced, a carrier of desiccation
from a well-whitewashed heaven.

## Nine Days

Semen and licorice smells.
Sea air smears

colors off the bald
backsides of houses on Poseidon Street.

I was coming from a broken
date at the cemetery: Adam's mother

was nine days dead, but all the other mourners
had left before the clammy pall of evening.

I had it to myself—
eleven oblongs, chummy chips of tile,

do-it-yourself with candles, snapshots, spades,
the old religion kit. I came to the doorless bone house.

Peeping in could one sense phosphorescence?
Too light still. Let's see, the new one. Fresh cement

is painted gray to look like fresh cement.
Earth, Adam's mother. Rib? Ceramics, merds.

Negative light. I thread my way back home
unmourning by the prows along the shore.

## Anonymous Birdwing

detached as a dotted line
decorative as our bone collection
yesterday was so much like tomorrow
I need landmarks, bookmarks, bonemarks,
totems of life or death
that blood-glued log now where
the white cock was beheaded
will do for a remembrance

octopus jerking spiderlike on the clothesline
fuss and crash of waves   birds in the wheat
spaced benediction of almond trees in bloom

adds up to what kind of beauty?
this great democracy of sun and water
wine and beer has been leaving me so lonely

habit is the ballast that keeps
the dog chained to his vomit
the best effecter of reconciliation
each hour becomes familiar as a gesture

stoop to scoop the water from the bucket
smooth your hair in automatic camouflage
someone is coming to gossip and the threshold
frames my disguise

## A Month After

Behind the mountain summer's banked fires die.
The harbor frieze blurs like a forgery.

Caiques have brought their cargoes from the islands,
donkeys and watermelons. We lack nothing.

The latest mainland visitor is courtly.
Never mind cloven hooves or syphilitic toenails.

Color of sea and sun, back bent to the rudder,
you slide your eyes over the watching windows,

careful pastels of houses built on rock,
then splash the searing indigo on me.

My mind has long had thought soaked out of it.
Let south wind wake a swell and break and drown us.

## *Dog Days*

One might try liver divination.
This season has no lack of animals freshly dead.

Lobes analyzed would only yield
what all this flesh keeps saying.

I was never accused of beauty
but nothing is left here but the body.

Yes, the hill blinkers
dawn a little if you get up early.

Yes, the merciful mountain hides it
half an hour sooner than the calendar says.

The Eye once opened, though, never winks for an instant.
Black-scarved women pound on the door like vengeance,

shattering calm of lecherous siestas.
Blue glare invades the slant of a mirror.

Zenith blazes. All the sea can do
is shrug back some of the light.

Only stars reel toward winter, but too slowly.

## Ἀγόρι μου Ψαρᾶ *

Crack village sinews! Sun
still sets behind the mountain,
boats rock at the limani,
but life is upside down.

A bitch killed thirty innocent
rabbits. Six turkeys pined and died.
Thanasis and the fat girl drowned.
Now the sponge fisherman went.

Cursed, the crones whisper. Swim
and you'll bump a bloated corpse.
We are punished for our sins.
I am punished for loving him.

Syrup of secret love has glazed my eyes.
I memorize your progress through the street
all day, I pace and play with cats at night.
For food I lick the sweetness of your lies.

From far away I'm scorched by your red shirt,
your golden body. An old homosexual hovers.
Every foreign girl is a ticket out.
I had forgotten just how love hurt.

From near, from far, you enter. This place
flexes its limbs, surrounds me.
Silence I'd basked in drowns me.
The eye of the storm is your unshaven face.

After all the moveless village is visited
by love and death. You might strangle me
in the blue proscenium of sea,
swim away, not turn your head.

Oh fill their waiting eyes,
the empty windows of the afternoons,
and dance me naked down Poseidon Street
before the sacrifice.

*Modern Greek: approximately* My boy, my fisherman

## Thalassa and the Villagers: A Vision

Slid out of bluish bushes the green snake,
but six or seven times and back to the slot,
dreamlike: finally got
across the lawn to where the white-faced girl
headed the villagers in single file.
First touched her ankles, twined around her thighs,
teeth to the love hole. Above, her eyes still blazed
in the dusk, but he ate her. Even the magic staff
she used for transformations was gone by morning,
dropped in the grass or devoured. The retinue
of villagers dispersed without a sound.

Only the white house at the end of the lawn
up on its bluffs went on confronting the sea,
defying weather, bones, and blood.
The grass was smooth enough to play croquet on.

The blaze-eyed girl had been so slender. Strange—
she might have been a mare the way he swelled,
the shining sated creature, but that day
he slid by secret tunnels back to the sea.

Remember, children, or the snake may eat you:
as color and light the whole sea may be drunk
as far as your eye can go to south, west, east,
Patmos, Fourni, Samiopoúla, see?
Only north is forbidden.

## Arson
### to Stavro

Hours and hours. I have heard the cry of the owl
and the Aegean washing and washing the stones
in the unfocused silence before dawn

too late. Twice the destroyer
ripped me out of sleep this same still hour.
It has burned a hole in the fabric of our days,

stamped a hot wound behind my closing eyelids.
So many moons and suns.
Did we think we had a share in all those risings?

The mountaintop flushed pink,
the chapel of Prophet Elijah flashed its beacon
message to Patmos, Leros,

donkeys, roosters, cats, caiques returning
and life picked up again
here on this beach that used to be plagued by pirates.

Danger, danger. The flames said it all.
Black-eyed holes reply in the night watches
to our not even breathed questions.

In this anarchic chilly space of time,
love, we are still together. Hold me, rock me.
Hush! Only the hunting owl.

The moon goes down, the bamboos crack,
the dog sighs in her curled sleep.
Another hour to wait

for intimations of day distinct from starlight,
two more for the blatant miracle itself:
our cue to dive back to the dark

region where fire may blaze, but heatless,
fists pound the door in silence
until twilight begins it again.

## *Two Sleepers*

In Vermont tornado
season you dreamed of waves.

My dream spun, a funnel,
picked up shapes and did away with them.

Kilted soldiers, a house, a field
wrenched out of this dimension.

You sighed and burrowed deeper.
South wind buffets the island.

Anathema of fishermen and swimmers,
it churns warm cloudy waves

nonsense of barriers, foam of obstacles.
The Customs Official composing

patriotic poems at his desk
will see salt marks on the threshold.

Women sweep away volcanic
rubble from Santorini,

all the trash that eddied in my mind
when you said you saw waves.

In the rain forest of the north
we wake to thunder.

Is it possible to miss that harrowing sun?
In the sad steam that's heat here can it be

that we will decide what to do with our lives?
Patience, you say, it will come.

I had forgotten the swarms of black flies
that enter the mouth like swallowed words.

## *Wintering*

overripe from the length of summer
sun sets off beyond the edge of the hill
nearly as possible motionless
my head against your shoulder
waiting for the deer's leap from the pines

the shared dream of fire
with memory in the north
we winterize our house
hot and cold as hunters
in their blaze-orange jackets

painting the poetess' house
whose husband blew his head off in the meadow
we watch for inner disorder
the child's drawing locked rooms
furniture huddled in exile

hot and cold as hunters
nearly as possible motionless
with the shared dream of fire
we winterize our house
poised in the dial of silences

## *Village Triptych*
### after Botticelli's *Three Miracles of Saint Zenobius*

Intent in this square of sunlight from the window
watching the color flow beneath my fingers
I remember the first glimmering long ago
of this world of burnished afternoons
in the Museum of the City of Imagination.

The same harsh clarity of angled color.
Next to the church of Saint Nektarios
dark squats the madman's door.

Arises the dead man from his cradle-coffin.
Outstretched arms of the saint, billowing robes
    in his hurry,
on to the next. The Mediterranean crowd
chorus backdrops skeptics worshippers
raw material of thaumaturgy
well grouped as ever sweeps by.
Dogs, donkeys watch it, docile.
Women and pigeons coo.
The background benediction is in church bells,
sparrows, color beneath my fingers,
sea unfailingly blue around the corner.

The central scene is the madman in the square
flanked and attended by weeping villagers
washed dressed caressed then bundled
into an ambulance
to be lanced of his ulcer in the capital.
His return in a day or two
smelly and blasphemous as ever
is still in the cartoon stage.

The sun goes down and saints and crowds depart.
Over abandoned walls whose chinks are full of flowers
next to the flat white glow of the evening church
I see the door of the little house. It closes.

### *Lear in Greece*\*

blue gray gritty orrid rox
a boy is piping among the time & assfiddles
here & there a tortoise

now before dawn the shadows
have the innocence of promise
a hooded maiden takes her father breakfast
work out the distance in cool gray blues
and pearly pinks and *ecco*
the sun comes up in glory
immensely bright, clearly pure

but English eyes are dazzled when Greek light,
harsh regent, takes possession   We retire
breakfast and correspondence at the inn

nothing in the world can equal
the bright yellow of these pines
O spaces in the hills O loneliness

speckled & spotted with various colours
& unmarkable tints

evening   O O light on the sea


\**Many phrases here are from comments Edward Lear scribbled on the landscape sketches he did while traveling in Greece.*

## *Weighing In*

It's almost time enough
for a complete skin change,
love, these five
years we've done together.

All that salt water
thirsty-making sun
eating sleeping waking
talking drinking thinking

slyly as a snake
has peeled a layer of life
body-shaped like skin
from our twin selves.

Your cheekbones jut,
bones are clothed with hardness.
I can still spare
a modicum of flesh.

Mutual nourishment,
marriage symbiotic?
Life has battened on us
or we on each other.

All those meals shared,
wine in copper measures,
leaning, heads together,
late into the evening

have sieved clear through and left us
changed, time-sculpted, fresh
as a sheet of paper
ready for new writing.

## *Dream Interpretation*

Great whales colored like cream whipped with blood
harpooned through tossed foam, singing
vertical leap through sleep.

Not a bad omen, says Mamà,
as long as no blood was oozing.
Only a mood, a color of the mind,
no death portended.

What about old Aslánis propped in his coffin
tucked in among roses, a napkin over his face,
shoes peeking tidily out at the end,
mouth gauzed to plug the death fluids?

That was a death that was to happen, my daughter.
No threnodies for the old.

Life then. This spring each morning in the garden
a screaking pump handle (UP and down UP down)
broke into dawn dreams
and in the glare of the east-facing window
we woke and looked at each other.

Such shapes, sounds, colors. Now I am without you,
what meat for the kaleidoscope?
Rose into blue of tenderness-anxiety,
yellow stab of doubt, old angry orange,
green green of this June park where I grew up,
phases of popsicle all spinning shift
raked by the croupier a palette takes shape

in its center
my thumb crooks the sudden eyehole
of your absence.

*Scherzo*
 *for CB*

Today your music difficultly makes
one of our separate uses of the morning

there valor on the hill
cutting a path through long-neglected pines
cultivating beyond our garden

difficult music bravely followed
wraps us in its diaphony

warp and woof of the rainbow
number the blades of grass
so: separate   so: in combination
so: so: again! and we at the ends of the lawn
unthanking woven in

difficult music valorously pursued
making our mornings one
what patterns past to present
down to this day, month, century,
what pavanes
all for the present exercise of glory

the roses on the bank can hardly help
opening their faces
blush colored to the heat

in harmony unsought
we cultivate our gardens

throw off your cloak in the sun
heroes of path-clearing
making your ways through twin forests
verticals horizontals
following opposing
signs to the rainbow's end

throw off your cloak in the sun
chill of delight is the heat that welds your motions
loving you may I say it
energy and beauty

what are you following
who hack your way through the forgotten pines?
who told you to clear a space among the ferns?
why do the roses open their morning faces?
what diggings in black earth
steps on what keyboard

YES all dragged like children
turning behind the terrible dear piper
we follow your difficult notes
now in the zenith
up to the rainbow whose arch spans all
our unthankfulness, all our loving.